Best Wishes to Margaret
—

Sincerely,
Elizabeth Fraser Williamson

Aug. 29/89

Toronto, Canada
Aug 28, 1989

THERE'S A LEGEND IN MY SPINE

THERE'S A LEGEND IN MY SPINE

SCULPTURES AND POEMS

OF

ELIZABETH FRASER WILLIAMSON

with photographs by Ernest Singer
and afterword by Gerry Moses

PENUMBRA PRESS, 1983

Inquiries regarding specifications and availability of
sculptures should be addressed to Elizabeth Fraser
Williamson at The Guild Inn, 201 Guildwood Parkway,
Scarborough, Ontario M1E 1P6.

Published by PENUMBRA PRESS, PO Box 340, Moonbeam,
Ontario P0L 1V0. Printed in Canada. The type is Garamond.

ISBN 0-920806-28-7 paper

for Fraser, Sara and Julia
with love

POETRY

SCULPTURE

far far back
and out of time
when the Phoenix
bending proud neck
of her own free will
struck the spark
lit the fire
was consumed ...
became amber ash
transmuted again
rose to tintinnabulation of hairbells
rose to fulness of being complete
each shining fluted feather
scintillating colour ...
at such a time — or out of it
a seed was dropped
dropped in the slumbering
heart of man
and then — O then — in a purple ribbed night
in the uttermost cave
of his being
blossomed a flower.
a small pale starlike flower
embryonic
but growing
expanding doubling trebling
shooting out petals buds branches
sending down roots
in a great rush

taking over man's whole interior
    rocking
    hammering his ribs
    riding the high tide
    of his breath
out out
in sheer explosion of joy ...
the rich-radiant tumultuous
trembling flower of love ...

and all was changed

9

UNICORN DAY

slowly
the Samurai Sun
swings
his glittering sword
this way and that
cutting and carving
the blazing blue —
and a bluejay flies
screaming in the dark wood
and I in a field
heavy with milkweed and mullen
fall,
dissolve,
flow into
veins of grass
where praying mantis
pale
translucent glass
wait
for shape and shadow
under a milkwhite moon

10

LEAVE TAKING

on the narrow bed
your long body
lies motionless
tired pulse
in skeletal throat

i note
the aching beauty
of bones
shining like whales
beneath stretched skin

you have not gone.
not yet —
you're there
within
behind closed eyes

i long
and stretch to find you
to be with you
warm you with love
till you go
tall and tree-like
down the narrow tunnel
of leave taking ...

12

MARCH MADNESS

the affectionate sun
nuzzles the bare neck
licks the cheek with warm tongue

i walk tall
trying to catch
the skyborne sound
of arrownecked geese
wedge-winging north:
magic since childhood
a wonder ritualed
from generation to
generation

along the puddled pavement
gaunt old hydro poles
pulsing thrumming
caroling to their narrow selves ...
reckless flinging ecstatic wires
heedless across a bell-toned sky
bloodtingling
sap ringing
crow cawing
madness!

14

AUGUST

the brassy sun
swung
and flung his molten mane
roaring his way to noon

and a small tree
gathered shade
prudently

while over the tilting ground
down sloping dry to seaward
a late-hunting fox
his golden brush
echo to golden sun
held firm between two pointed ear
an image sure
of den and dark
and earth sweet sleep

15

AMPHIBIAN

You see a human
lying sunstretched
on rock near water.

It looks like me. It is not.

I have been transformed.
Heat pouring like lava
has stirred some primal
part of my being.
I am back back in time
to giant lizards
and slow-moving reptiles.

I am part of them. I am amphibian.

Stretched prone. Heat filling
every pore every eager cell
dragon-tongues licking
along chill veins.

I crave heat unlimited.

Inner sigh proclaims
the body's need and greed
for sun is slaked.
I inch belly forward
reach the rock's lip
slither down

entering water
without sound or ripple.

Cruise ...
Cruise like whale
in elemental world
I once knew. Diving
deeper and deeper
into silence
into darkening green
the sun   a faraway flower
raying petals palely
toward black alchemist
world of acquatic creatures.

And I   only part.

Without learning I fish-swim
lazy motion effortless power.

Power attacks. Body twists
spirals upward
full throttle
undulating sealfashion
to break surface
and greet the air   the sun
with most unseal-like

Shout!

17

AFTER THE LATE GUEST WAS GONE

After the late guest was gone
he leaned upon the winter wind
slowly sipped the icy stars
curled against the ribs of night
and slept the sleep
of the northern hare

19

INDIAN MASK

Not just a mask
but a Presence;
indwelling presence
with memory
of sun-stabbed woods,
of hills like petroglyphs
scrawled across
the limestone sky,
and with the earth's
slow turn
comes memory of snow
soft falling snow
covering a race
of silenced people
under.

20

IN THE HOUR AFTER LOVE

In the hour after love
she rose from the bed,
left his slumbering form
walked naked-foot
into the woods.

Pent-energy
rose in full flood
till in a fury
she seized a birch
snapped it in two
and clubbed the waning moon
till it crept whimpering
into a torn shroud of cloud.

After that
she slept in the glimmer
of white violets
the moon snuggled nicely
between her breasts.

22

THE CHILD WAKENS

the child wakens.
awareness
of heartbeat and bloodtide
of pulsing sap
breathing grass
the utter wholeness
of all things
trees
stones
mountains ...
and the morning
brings forth fruit
round to the point
of marvel

and the child
bursting with joy
leaps from bed
bounds through the door
(knocking the teacup
from his mother's hand)
and escapes —
a furious windmill
of arms and legs
barrelling
into the beckoning
day

NINA

with mindfree ease
the hawk enscribes
circles in the glass sky
air flowing through feathers
as water through fins of fish

in a morning meadow
deep in daisies
Nina stands
yearning hawkward
sunburned limbs light as leaves
as spirit leaps to joy of soaring
and the whole free clear sphere
of sky and bird and Nina.

25

NIGHTMARE

at the bus-stop restaurant
a lion
crouches on the counter
between ketchup and mustard
calmly munching
the straw-coloured hair
of a small girl
who stares
with wide oyster eyes
as terror chews
her heart

and I and others
turn to stone.

26

TO A PRE-NATAL PERSON

did you feel
a double tide
when short days
before your birth
your mother calmly
swam
with wide frog-like
motion?
did you then
feel the rise and fall
in your own private ocean?

28

FALLEN TREE

my caressing hand
        explores
the round smooth
slow curving flank
        happens
on a sudden hole
arm sized and deep
antenna fingers
        probe
feel grass lined walls
        hair soft
then thrusting twisting
        farther back
        invade
the cupped hidden world
of blind-throbbing
        babybirds

29

DIANNE

you
clearcut finely honed
steel wire stretched
precisely
between star points

you
luminous moth
sorceress
cradling furry creatures
staring through owl eyes
beauty like curved talons
polished
perfect for purpose

you
shadow sharp
on clipped grass
blurring on millpond
scattering amongst chatter
of lilac leaves
shadow lengthening
deepening
growing gargantuan
becoming
mountain of fear
a bear to be wrestled
till dawn
cries truce

JOY IN THE SUMMER DUST

along the country road
she went
light and bright
as peony petals —
floating joy

joy nibbled her heels
and they leapt like lambs
bouncing in small bounces
spurts of joy in the
summer dust.
'one must fly' she thought
'must eagle soar
in the milkblue sky'
and her heels drummed joy
in the summer dust

buttercups sang!
joy rang from tall elms
rang so strident clear
the tremulous glass
of her heat broke
in tinkling fragments
of splintered joy.

and her heels drummed joy
in the summer dust

AT LEAST AS LONG

I loved you loved you
Loved you
Took your name
From the hidden box
Of my heart
Wrote it with care
On the wet sands
Of the Upper Ottawa

When evening came
And I saw your name
Had washed away
I waded deep
Wrote your name again
In water
So it would last
At least as long
As the Upper Ottawa.

CHRISTMAS, 1975

like blurred speech
the landscape
slurred
by falling snow
trees gone wraiths
in gentle breathing night

Julia in Alashstar
in Luristan
in the warm purple mountains
of Iran:
under the dark
tunnel of night
if snowflakes fell
they'd be
laughing
frozen tears

33

THERE'S A LEGEND IN MY SPINE

There's a legend in my spine.
dimly felt
waiting

On nights of
waxing moon
it moves like shadow.
passing through
fingerbones
into clay.

There's a legend in my spine
waiting

34

GENTLY IT COMES

gently it comes
like the first
hesitant drops of rain —
a feeling of soaring

it comes
when I watch trees
tallstanding together
lifting limbs
to touch lightly
one to the other

it comes
when a gull
dark against pale sky
tilts a wing sunward
in slowcurving glide

it comes, the feeling of soaring
flowing into fetal clay
that under sculpting hands
sighs
and waits to grow

36

INVOCATION I

I have not slept,
Not eaten,
Drank only the water
Spirit of the lake —
And my spirit
Thin as the new moon
Grows sharp with hunger
With yearning.

O Stone!
White as the loon's throat —
Hear me:
"Indwelling Spirit!"
Flow from the sacred caverns of our race
Flow from the bright Spirit World —
Enter the dark tent of my being
Fill me with Light!"

for the film "Spirit of Stone"

37

INVOCATION II

Now to this place
in the dawn I come
clean in spirit
marrow
bone
drawn from the earth
the trees
and the mountain
the strength and the soul
of this sacred stone.

39

After the magic of snow
Sacred Bull
lifted the full power
of his horns
impaling the trembling tree
who tried
to pierce the winter moon!

Everything has a place that seems more "right" than others. As soon as Sacred Bull was born I knew the clue to his right place lay in the curve of his horns. That great sweeping arc must frame something significant. I found it in the background of tall ash trees. The Bull is a combination of wisdom and gentleness while the trees between his horns make their own vertical statements about life.

FALLING TOTEM

Deep in the moss hushed woods
the totem leans
earthward
imperceptibly falling
in dream motion
slowly
inch by slow inch
till in a year
or ten
it sudden crashes
through fragile ferns
down
down to dark alchemist
world of worm
and root
and seed

42

THE SEARCHER

When night invades
the woods
she moves like shadow
sleek body
stretching contracting
shape-changing
flowing
round stones
logs
silking softly
through briar
searching
seeking small
frightened
innocent
things
furred and feathered
dropping them into
pockets of sleep
murmuring
'putting my woods to bed ...'

soundless
singular
unseen
Searcher

44

WELL AND SMOOTHLY BORN

He became aware
first of himself
then of something pending.
His bright spirit waited
crouched within
the neat bundle
of birdlike bones
and rounded flesh.

He arrived gently
carried on a wave
from private pond
to alien shore.
He filled his lungs.
He spoke loudly.
Felt the heart-drum
and knew he was home.

He melted into
the bliss of breast
of milk and love
flowing copiously
the round moon
of mother-face close by.

Presently the full-milk sigh
and deep tidal sleep
of one who is well
and smoothly born.

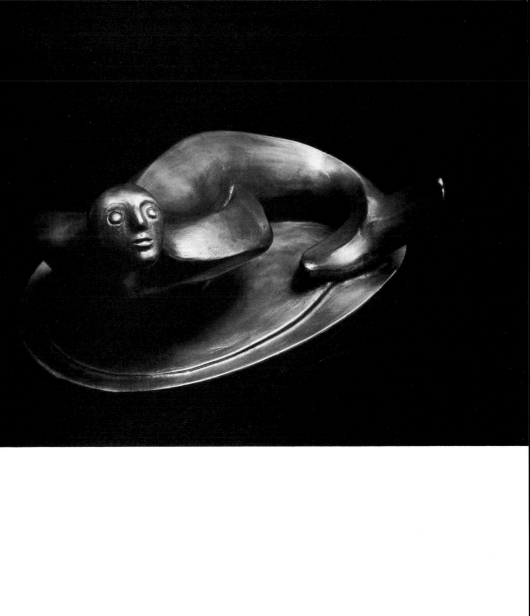

JULIA AND CHILD

Young woman seated
On the floor
Encircles laughing child —
Happiness
Rapport

48

What is she doing there — what?
Standing alone and so lonely
Worn to the bone
Yet strong —
Supporting her one and her only.

*With this piece, the woman was at first splendidly
pregnant, the important part being the full rich swelling
in the middle. Gradually, however, as I carved the back
the natural depression between shoulder blades and
down the spine opened up. At the same time a similar
thing was happening to the torso in front. Eventually
her body opened up completely, the bony walls letting
in light and air in a pleasant way.*

*She then seemed to me to be both pregnant and
delivered. Her arms still circle round the unborn child
as if to support the weight. Yet now the child is not
only born, but standing in front of his mother reaching
up to her. From one angle the mother's hand becomes
the child's head, from another angle, the child has
disappeared completely.*

*It was not till some time after completion that the
image of the Biblical Hagar came to mind.*

50

WINDSWEPT

Shapes
like sound go round
and round and upward
mount on joyswept wings.

52

SAMURAI

concentration on the inner eye
        warrior spirit
           samurai!

SPIRIT

she floats through wide unchartered space
        feels with the wind
        keens with the wind
        heals with the wind
           the night-torn faces.

Dual aspects of single sculpture.

53

Following Plates:
SAMURAI
SAMURAI SPIRIT

TENDERNESS

So much in love these two!
Even the space between is filled
With tenderness —
They are a pair even when apart.

56

GENTLE PROMPTINGS

They follow with their hearts
the promptings of the Tall One.

58

LISTEN CAREFULLY

... then he called them to him
and placing his arms round about
drew them close
and a great stillness
fell upon the three ...
"Listen carefully _____"

60

WOMB FOR THE WEARY

Space
peers round
and is curious.
Flowing forms
folding inward —
womb for the weary.

62

MOON GOD

Fierce stubborn proud
this granite face.
Before I carved
he already existed!

64

ESKIMO WOMAN

Standing firm as a granite rock
Heart as warm as healing rain
Woman finds her inner strength
Freely — gives it out again.

66

NIGHT AND DAY

In one sinuous twist of time
Rising day and dying night
Flow together

68

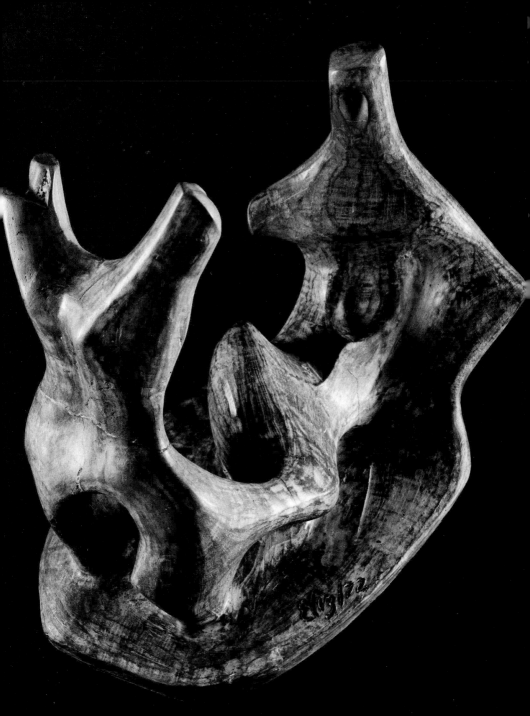

JULIA SLEEPING

A magician came upon a sleeping woman.
So serene, remote and utterly beautiful was
she that he desired to see her thus forever.
He changed her into a stone, then flung
the stone into the sky where it became
the Moon — serene, remote and utterly
beautiful forever.

70

PILLAR OF PROTEST

lifting blind face to heaven
stubborn she stands —
pillar of protest
screaming demands.

72

A WILY SHAMAN

He came from
Thunderheads
and
the thick black
shadows
under the spruce

His face bone-strong
features curved
like claws
eyes
deep pools unfathomed
mirth flickering
at mouth corners

A wily Shaman

a brooding spirit
smelling of mountains
gathering stones
to his moon-drenched
soul.

74

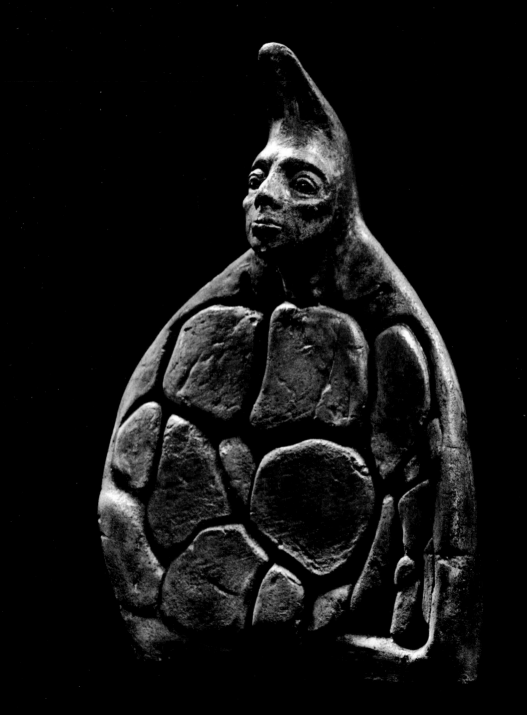

not what I say
not the black words
on the white page
but the stems of trees
grey against still snow
caught in the mirror of a room

❦

An idea, like a seed
sown at the right moment ...
how incalculable the growth!

❦

My mind needs others
To rub against.
Corners crumble
new shapes appear.

❦

Through will,
stray thoughts
are brought to heel —
Alas! not so the heart!

❦

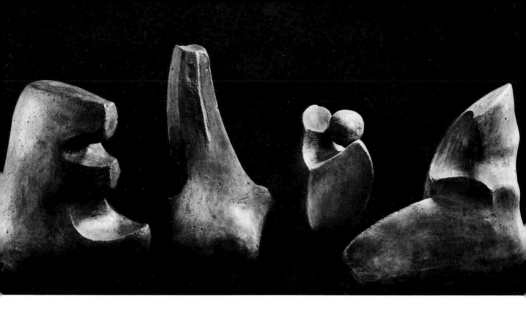

winter trees
devour the moon
nibbling its bright edges
with sharp black teeth

&

pre-cambrian hills:
glacial thumbprints
smudged across the sky.

&

A tree and a person
must grow —
do not bend the branch.

&

transparent moth
fluttering vaguely
under the sun.
O to see you
luminous strong
under the moon!

&

78

through canyons of clouds
like scraps of burnt paper
crows are riding the autumn winds

❧

As solitary as a loon
on a northern lake —
so the pierced heart.

❧

From his measured mind
he took words
like pebbles chosen
for perfect shape.

❧

the day is huge with promise
it pushes feathers
into my bones
      i am light.
      i walk like
      a moth hovering
      over a flower
i draw slow circles
round my thoughts
bid them be still ...
      the day remains promiseful
      and will if i swim
      the sacred stream
      roll the entire universe
      under the small hollow
      of my hand

80

Following Plates:
DEEP THOUGHT
STONE MANTLE
ANIMAL GIVING BIRTH
LEANING ON GENTLE STRENGTH
NEW BORN
BOY AND BIRD SET SAIL
TIBETAN LAMAS
ANCIENT KING
THE ATHLETE
LADY UNICORN
ORGANIC ABSTRACT
BUDDHA HEAD

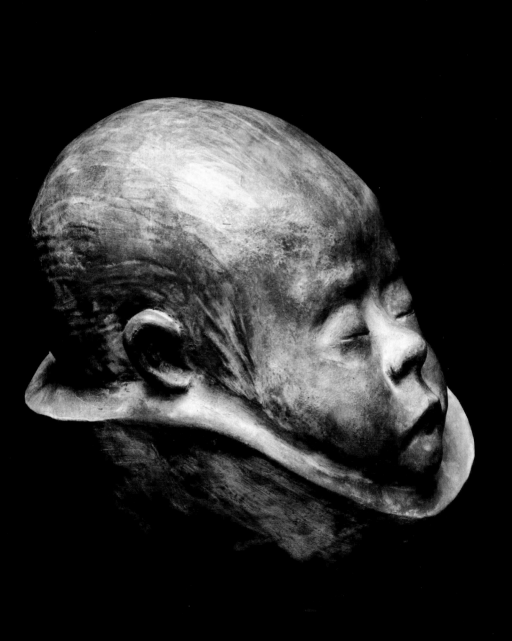

AFTERWORD, *by Gerry Moses*

The viewing of art is the end of a magic process. What we see and what we listen to, have come from a magic nowhere; the nowhere that artists seem to know, a magic world outside the world we know. Yet when we face the work of art we somehow join that world; somehow seem carried back; somehow remember vaguely as if we too had once been there.

The works of Elizabeth Fraser Williamson are friendly works, works that invite recall; recall of dreams, hints of inspiration, of time past, of time to come and within the magic, of time outside of time.

She is one of those intuitive artists who of necessity rather than preference plucks her inspiration from the quiet backwaters of experience rather than from the fashionable and racy changeability of current trends. She is very much her own person and thus her art is very much her own.

Born of an innocence obviously cherished from childhood wonder, a fascination for myth and an intimate identification with nature, her subjects appear miraculously from the fondling touch of hand to clay. They come of their own accord at their own time. She welcomes them, embraces them when they appear, coaxes them to remain and finally assume the form they take, especially for her.

94

They appear from her own unconscious, a step at a time, sometimes with only the slightest hint by accident perhaps appearing in the clay. Sometimes to tease, remaining just beyond the grasp of recognition, only to recede again returning unidentified to the mystery of the creative process.

But then again sometimes the hint becomes a lighted way and inspiration has an easy birth, a new being comes to earth, perhaps in form, or mask, a head or figure, perhaps a spirit person, an animal or bird.

It seems they come when they must come first in the vagueness of the artist's dream. Then released to air from clay, they by seeming magic of the sculptor's touch appear and once appeared are held for us the viewer to enjoy and hold dialogue.

Intuitive rhythms dominate the sculpture of Elizabeth Fraser Williamson, some spatial in origin, some organic in their derivation. The subject matter seems to dictate choice and feeling.

The sculptures carry an aura of gentleness. Tensions and contrasts within the works are usually quiet and are never allowed much rein of conflict. When energies infer a confrontation they diffuse in change of rhythms. Finally they return within and are contained, or are released in accent addressed to the world outside.

95

The rhythms dictate the final form in which they are themselves contained. They are the life and presence of each work. They reflect the subject matter which has its origin elsewhere.

Elizabeth Fraser Williamson never loses touch with the essential soul of the subject and builds around it the mystery and magic of her own vision.

To know this work is to touch the wonder of the woods, the inner soul of trees and the lively gentleness of man.

Toronto, May 1, 1983

96